What is... ARBOR DAY

Find our books at Amazon, Barnes & Nobles, Walmart, Books-A-Million, OverDrive, Kobo, Lulu and more!

Like, Share and Follow us on Facebook, Instagram, Twitter, Pinterest, YouTube, LinkedIn, Spotify, Apple Podcast and more!

Sloth Dreams Publishing

www.SlothDreamsBooks.com

www.SlothDreamsBooks.com

Published by Sloth Dreams Books & Publishing
Sloth Dreams Children's Books
Pennsylvania, USA
www.SlothDreamsBooks.com

ISBN: 978-6-1145-7113-1

What is... ARBOR DAY

by KeriAnne Jelinek

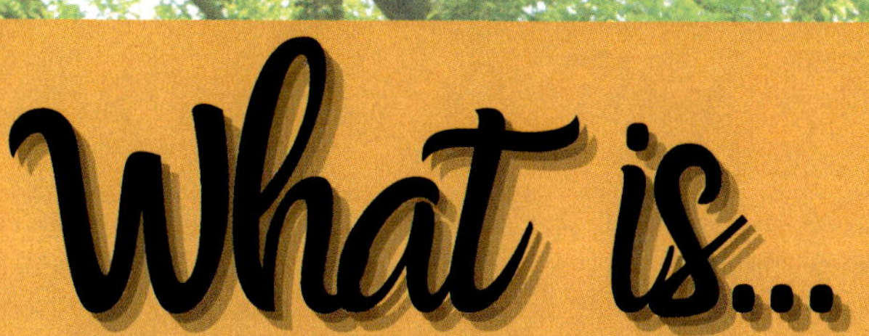

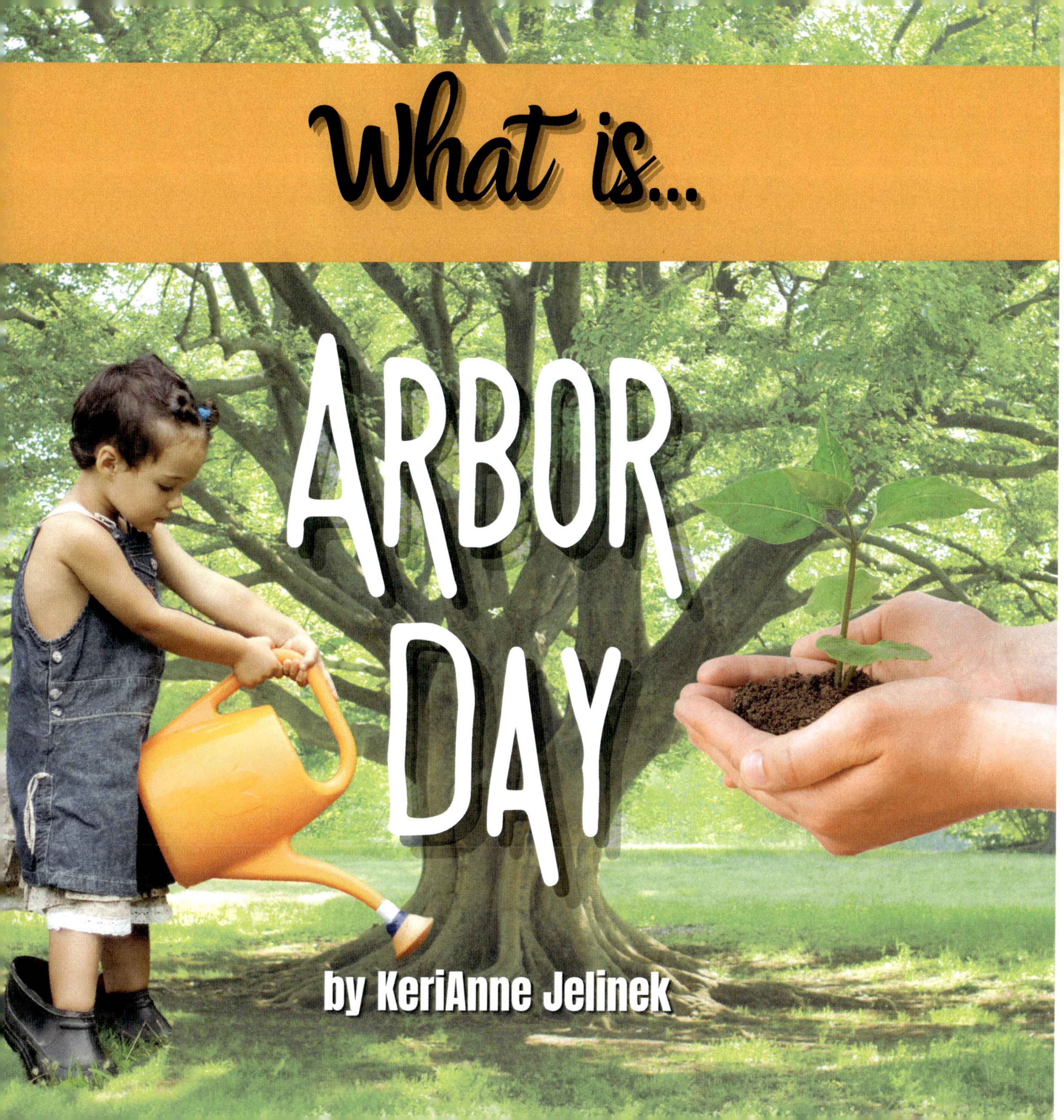

What is Arbor Day?

Arbor Day is a nationally celebrated holiday that began in 1874. "Arbor" Day, meaning "tree" day, is a day that has been set aside to protect preserve and plant trees.

The first Arbor Day originated with a man named J. Sterling Morton. He was a tree enthusiast that loved trees. Morton was a Nebraska newspaper editor. He took his idea of planting trees to the Nebraska City State Board of Agriculture meeting that was held in Lincoln, NE. He advocated for people and groups to plant trees. He first proposed a tree planting holiday at that meeting in January of 1872.

The tree planting day was set for April 10, 1872. Over one million trees were planted in Nebraska on that first special Arbor Day. It was officially set as a state holiday in 1874 by Robert W. Furnas, the Nebraska Governor. Later in 1885 it was named a legal state holiday for Nebraska. The holiday is typically held the last week of April, and is a different date each year, despite it having been permanently set for April 22.

Later, a man by the name of Birdsey Northrop took the concept of planting trees and promoted it nationwide, to Japan, Canada, Australia and even Europe. He is responsible for the Arbor Day becoming a globalized initiative.

At the beginning of 1906, a man by the name of Major Israel McCreight, of DuBois, Pennsylvania urged President Theodore Roosevelt to make a public statement to school-aged children about trees. He urged the President to talk about the destruction of forests in the United States.

During this time, there were many lumber companies tearing down forests all across America. McCreight was a strong opponent of the lumber industry tearing down trees. McCreight recommended to President Roosevelt a progressive campaign for tree and forest conservation for youth. President Roosevelt, on April 15, 1907, gave an Arbor Day proclamation to the children around the world. The proclamation stated the importance of forest conservancy, and the importance of trees and safe forestry. Roosevelt proclaimed that schools in the United States deserved to benefit from being educated about forestry and trees.

Since the first Arbor Day in April, 1872 many countries around the world have since adopted the holiday. Australia, Belgium, Brazil, British Virgin Islands, Cambodia, Canada, Central African Republic, China, Republic of Congo, Costa Rica, Cuba, Czech Republic, Egypt, Germany, India, Iran, Israel, Japan, Kenya, Korea, Lesotho, Luxembourg, Malawi, Mexico, Mongolia, Namibia, Netherlands, New Zealand, Niger, North Macedonia, Pakistan, Phillippines, Poland, Portugal, Russia, Samoa, Saudi Arabia, South Africa, Spain, Sri Lanka, Tanzania, Uganda, United Kingdom, United States, and Venezuela all have their own Arbor Day or Tree Planting Days.

Just as the first Arbor Day started with just one person, we can also make a difference one tree and one person at a time. We can plant new trees and find new ways to conserve the trees we still have.

What can we do to
celebrate and participate
in Arbor Day?

We can
plant a tree
in our own
backyard.

We can join a community
or group tree planting
committee.

We can advocate for the
safe and ethical removal of
diseased or dead trees.

We can support laws and politicians that promote tree and forest conservation.

We can save trees and our
environment by choosing
alternative ways to heat our
homes. Burning wood is
dangerous for the ozone
around our planet and is
not a sustainable energy
source for the
environment.

We can buy products, homes and materials that do not support the deforestation of trees. Cutting down trees and forests destroys animal habitats, and depletes oxygen the trees make so we can breathe.

We can choose
to not buy or
promote
Christmas
trees that have
been cut down
from forests.

We can support forest conservation organizations and groups, such as, Sierra Club, TREE Foundation and other organizations.

We can learn and read about our local forests and our global forests.

We can choose to use recycled materials instead of using wood products in our home.

ZERO
WA
STE

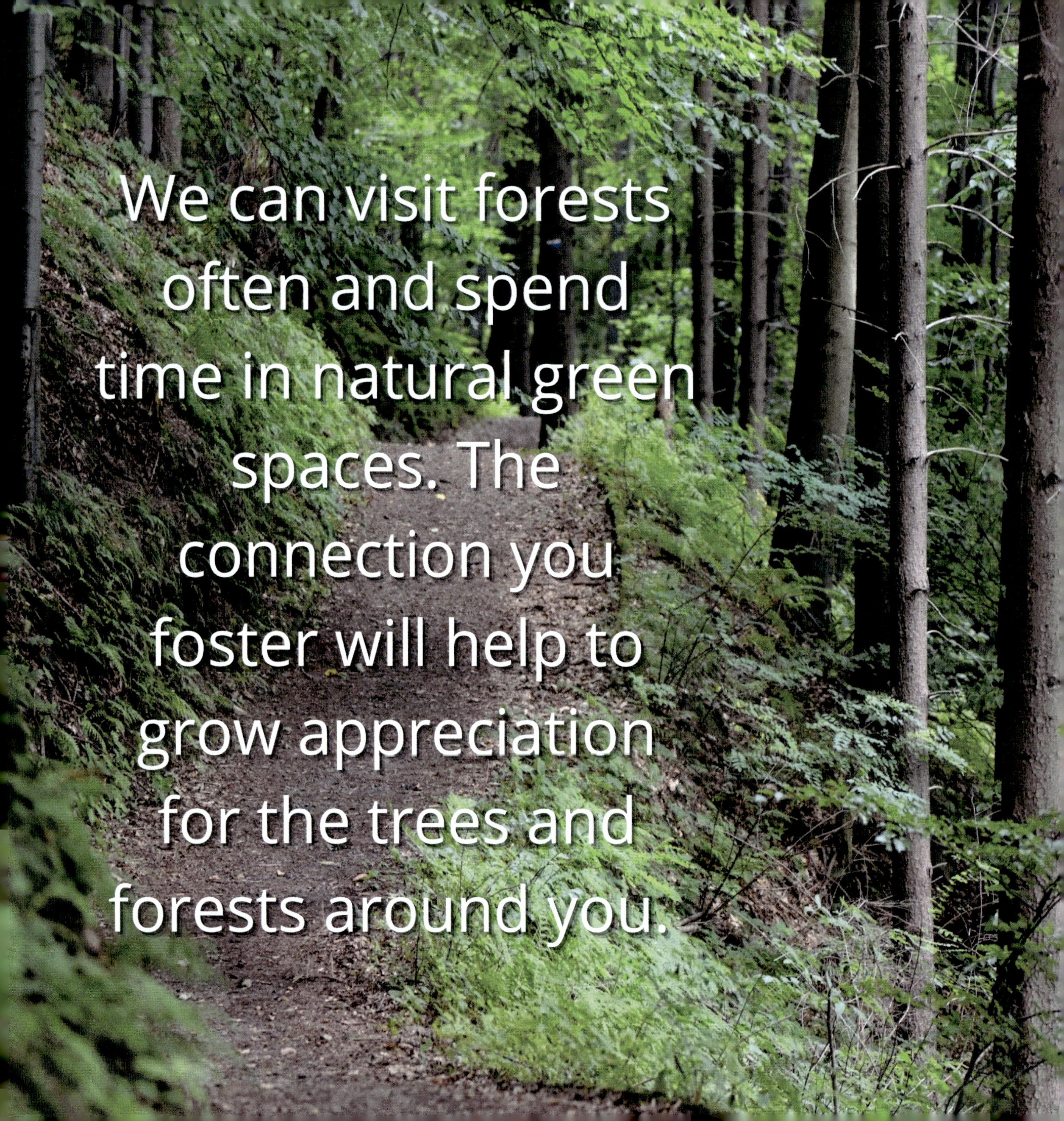

We can visit forests often and spend time in natural green spaces. The connection you foster will help to grow appreciation for the trees and forests around you.

We can go hiking, have a picnic, go camping, or even try to climb a tree. The connection to nature will increase our personal well-being, health and positive mental health.

We can support indigenous people as they fight to keep trees protected from large corporations trying to take away their lands.

We can learn and teach others about forests through outdoor exploration and exploring books about trees.

Whether tall or small, young or old, we all have an obligation to protect our wonderful trees. Arbor Day starts with us. One small change can grow into bigger changes that lead to environmental conservation for trees. Every little thing you do today helps our environment and trees tomorrow.

Every person doing their part will lead to a healthier planet, safer environment and a more beautiful Earth filled with trees. Let's help keep our Earth beautiful with trees one person at a time!

Made in the USA
Las Vegas, NV
05 December 2024

13429329R00026